The Art of Critical Thinking

The Art of Critical Thinking

Avalon March

CONTENTS

- Introduction — 1
- 1 Understanding Critical Thinking — 3
- 2 Developing Analytical Skills — 5
- 3 Enhancing Problem-Solving Abilities — 7
- 4 Evaluating Evidence and Arguments — 9
- 5 Recognizing Logical Fallacies — 11
- 6 Applying Critical Thinking in Decision-Making — 13
- 7 Improving Creative Thinking — 16
- 8 Overcoming Cognitive Biases — 19
- 9 Enhancing Communication Skills — 22
- 10 Cultivating Curiosity and Open-Mindedness — 25
- 11 Utilizing Critical Thinking in Research and Analys — 28
- 12 Promoting Ethical Reasoning — 31
- 13 Fostering Collaborative Thinking — 34

14 | Applying Critical Thinking in Everyday Life 37

| Conclusion 40

| Enjoyed This Book? Let Others Know! 42

Copyright © 2025 by Avalon March
All rights reserved. No part of this book may be reproduced in any manner whatsoever without written permission except in the case of brief quotations embodied in critical articles and reviews.
First Printing, 2025

Introduction

The Art of Critical Thinking unfolds in four segments, each meticulously crafted to guide readers through a transformative cognitive journey:

1. **Part I: Introduction to Critical Thinking** This segment serves as the foundation for developing conscious, deliberate thought through practice. It delves into six critical aspects of continuous improvement, explores the role of dependent and independent variables in discussions, and introduces the T.O.D. (Think, Observe, Decide) method. Additionally, it offers two key strategies to navigate and neutralize negative communication derailments while laying the groundwork for problem-solving essentials.
2. **Part II: Re-Educating the Educators** This section is a call to action for educators, empowering them to seamlessly integrate problem-solving and critical thinking skills into classroom environments. It identifies the barriers that often hinder critical thinking and provides actionable, practical solutions to overcome these challenges.
3. **Part III: Exploring Problem-Solving in Depth** This segment takes a focused dive into problem-solving. Each critical aspect is analyzed with a clear definition, supported rationale, and effective strategies. Using Rubric One, participants gain tools to formulate solutions rooted in certainty. Techniques like guided imagery, attention to physical displays, and intentional gestures enhance the clarity and confidence of conclusions.

4. **Part IV: Comprehensive Application through a Think Tank** The final segment ties the journey together by summarizing key elements of critical thinking. It facilitates an experiential learning environment through participation in a "Think Tank." This collaborative approach enables participants to synthesize their learnings and design robust professional development plans, preparing them to foster critical thinking in various professional contexts.

To think competently is to think critically. **The Art of Critical Thinking** prioritizes the development of cognitive skills that elevate intelligence across disciplines and subject matters. This transformation is the true beauty of critical thinking—it transitions you from merely receiving information to becoming an empowered individual who defines problems, generates innovative solutions, and eliminates the noise of self-doubt and anxiety.

This workshop provides a framework to embrace catalytic change as a constant companion. By mastering critical thinking, you gain the tools to create mutually beneficial, long-lasting effects, both professionally and personally.

1

Understanding Critical Thinking

The second stage of critical thinking revolves around cultivating the skill to reject thoughts that diverge from reality. This discipline, once nurtured, becomes a cornerstone of cognitive maturity. Young adults often describe the emergence of this ability as a profound understanding, especially when it stems from the interplay of other essential cognitive skills. A precise grasp of reality requires intellectual courage—the willingness to confront and accept our own cognitive weaknesses. This courage is the gateway to embarking on the lifelong journey of self-knowledge.

Metaphorically, we are often our own worst critics, scrutinizing our thoughts as though shielding our vulnerabilities. However, this self-critique, when approached constructively, is not a weakness but an opportunity for growth. By awakening our creativity and constructing coherent thoughts, we move beyond the realm of what merely feels reasonable. Instead, we embrace conclusions that emerge from the rigorous interplay of logic and evidence—a harmony where our thinking aligns with the phenomenon at hand.

Critical thinking empowers us to derive knowledge not just from the conclusions we reach but also from the premises that underpin them. When we analyze and verify that these premises accurately mirror reality, we can trust that our conclusions hold truth. In this way, critical thinking serves as a system of metacognition—a process of thinking about thinking—that sharpens our ability to reason effectively.

The foundational stage of critical thinking lies in self-recognition: the ability to identify and evaluate our own thought processes to determine their validity. This stage demands a deliberate decision and commitment to two pivotal groups of cognitive skills: a) The ability to discern between our own thoughts and those of others, ensuring originality and independent reasoning. b) The capacity to evaluate when our thinking aligns with objective reality, fostering intellectual honesty and precision.

By mastering these skills, we empower ourselves to approach reality with clarity and confidence. Critical thinking is not merely a tool for solving problems—it is an art form that refines how we perceive, interpret, and engage with the world around us.

2

Developing Analytical Skills

The subject of critical thinking has been extensively explored in literature, with nearly every book on the topic offering its own conception or definition. These definitions, often brief and sometimes presented in lists, serve as concise summaries of critical thinking's essence. However, more comprehensive and wide-ranging definitions should incorporate essential components that enhance understanding and practical application.

One of these components is the **content-level indicator**, which characterizes the depth of substantive analysis while fostering an inquisitive and democratic mindset. This type of definition contrasts with content analysis, the process of identifying and correcting the misleading or superficial implications of a statement. For instance, in *De Finibus' Critical Thinking*, significant emphasis is placed on engaging deeply with cultural heritage—a subject that exemplifies the richness of analytical exploration.

At its core, there is a singular skill that all individuals who have completed advanced education should master with both precision and poise. This indispensable skill is the ability to analyze statements and critically evaluate the reasoning underpinning them. Such a procedure, while integral to formal contexts, extends its relevance to practical, everyday affairs. Whether in professional environments or personal interactions, the application of this skill shapes how we interpret, respond to, and navigate the complexities of our world.

The methodology of critical thinking achieves its full scope only when these dual aspects—**statement analysis** and **critical evaluation of arguments**—are integrated seamlessly. Statement analysis involves breaking down the structure of a statement, identifying its key components, and assessing their alignment with factual reality. Meanwhile, critical evaluation examines the strength of the arguments, probing their assumptions, logic, and potential biases.

By honing these analytical skills, critical thinking transforms into a pervasive methodology that transcends mere academic exercises. It becomes a tool for navigating and interpreting the nuances of both formal intellectual pursuits and the intricate dynamics of everyday decision-making. This blend of depth and practicality illustrates the profound impact of analytical reasoning when fully realized.

3

Enhancing Problem-Solving Abilities

Problem-solving is rooted in the intricate web of multilayered knowledge structures that we build over a lifetime. These structures emerge through the consolidation of experiences, ideas, and learned strategies, forming a dynamic cognitive map. This map becomes the launchpad for approaching solutions. However, these structures do not solidify solely through the accumulation of knowledge; their strength is determined by the quality of our problem-solving interactions.

The most effective problem-solving strategies are those we instinctively recall and rely on. As we revisit and apply these strategies to uncover solutions, they become increasingly refined and embedded in our cognitive framework. Over time, the recurring use of these strategies instantiates them into enduring mental constructs.

A fascinating phenomenon in problem-solving is **transfer**, where strategies developed for one problem can be adapted to address another. This ability to generalize problem-solving methods across contexts is a hallmark of cognitive flexibility. Each successful resolution reinforces the recall of these strategies, embedding them deeper into our memory and enabling their application to similar challenges with increasing efficiency.

Yet, as a society, we have become overly reliant on medications or external cognitive aids, often treating them as catch-all solutions. This dependence has eroded essential problem-solving skills, leaving us less adept at leveraging our natural associative abilities. Many intelligent organisms, such as dogs and chimpanzees, instinctively employ critical thinking and adaptive aids to navigate challenges—an ability humans are capable of but have not consistently nurtured.

The essence of effective problem-solving lies in critical examination. When approached systematically, every problem becomes a stepping stone toward its resolution. However, numerous habits cultivated over time have dulled our capacity for cognitive exploration.

Consider the innate curiosity of a child. Children instinctively question the world around them—why the sun rises and sets, why the earth isn't flat, why the sky is blue. This sense of wonder ignites new mechanics in their cognitive processes as they make connections between seemingly unrelated ideas. As we learn and engage with our senses, these connections spark the creation of new conceptual "nodes," building pathways that allow for associative relationships to form.

Sophisticated problem-solving strategies aim to order these connections, bringing structure to our conceptual maps. By aligning disparate ideas and experiences into a coherent framework, problem-solving transforms chaos into clarity. It is this process that equips us to approach problems not just with precision, but with creativity and adaptability.

Ultimately, the art of problem-solving is more than just a skill—it is a way of thinking. By refining our ability to analyze, associate, and adapt, we regain the cognitive agility that propels us toward innovative solutions.

4

Evaluating Evidence and Arguments

In evidence-driven fields, the focus shifts from merely memorizing facts to critically analyzing and interpreting evidence. These disciplines emphasize the idea that knowledge is not static but is constructed through the careful evaluation of evidence. Students are taught to see how their learning emerges as a process of building scientific, historical, or psychological theories from the ground up.

What better way to demonstrate this than by immersing students in the methodologies of these fields? By actively engaging in scientific experiments, historical investigations, or psychological observations, students not only develop their own conclusions but also experience the process of creating knowledge. This approach is not only more engaging but also nurtures a sense of ownership—students value conclusions they've derived themselves far more than those they've simply memorized. At its core, education thrives when students, rather than teachers, take the lead in creating and shaping knowledge.

As we embark on the journey of knowledge creation, vast amounts of evidence and data are accumulated. This evidence can stem from a variety of sources—systematic research methods, informal observations, intuition, or even casual opinions. Yet, not all evidence is created equal, and the challenge lies in evaluating this abundance with discernment. We cannot afford to treat all evidence with the same weight; doing so risks compromising the integrity of our conclusions.

In many cases, conflicting pieces of evidence must be weighed against one another to determine their relevance and credibility. This requires critical thinking—the skill of systematically analyzing evidence and the arguments derived from it. Often, the evaluation process goes beyond the evidence itself and extends to assessing the validity of the arguments being made. Critical thinking lies at the very heart of rationality, truth, and wisdom, serving as the foundation for sound reasoning.

True critical thinking emerges when students are encouraged to think deeply about evidence and arguments. By examining their premises and evaluating their logical coherence, students can distinguish strong, evidence-based conclusions from weak or fallacious ones. This analytical approach transforms learning into a dynamic and transformative process, where the pursuit of truth becomes both an intellectual and creative endeavor.

In essence, the ability to critically evaluate evidence and arguments is a cornerstone of critical thinking. It not only shapes how we approach knowledge but also prepares us to engage meaningfully with the world, armed with clarity, precision, and a deep commitment to intellectual integrity.

5

Recognizing Logical Fallacies

A fallacy is, at its core, a false or mistaken idea. Like the term "theory," "fallacy" is broad, encompassing a range of misconceptions and errors in reasoning. The concept can sometimes be made unnecessarily complex through the addition of convoluted adjectives that create a kaleidoscope of linguistic confusion. For students, the challenge of untangling this expanding terminology can feel overwhelming, leading to frustration rather than clarity.

Instead of approaching fallacies as an exercise in linguistic or logical dexterity, this chapter seeks to frame the topic as a straightforward exploration. The goal is to foster understanding, rather than bewilderment, through the application of logical acumen. Philosophically, the concept of a fallacy extends beyond formal logic; it represents a "problem" rooted in flawed reasoning, often influenced by external factors or context.

To make the study of logical fallacies more manageable, it is useful to group them into categories. This structured approach facilitates learning and aids in memorization, providing a clear framework for navigating the intricacies of flawed reasoning. While there may be some disagreement among scholars regarding the classification of all fallacies, certain patterns emerge as fundamental and can be heuristically outlined for quick reference and practical use.

Familiarity with common logical fallacies is a powerful tool in critical thinking. Recognizing patterns of faulty reasoning enables us to avoid falling into these traps ourselves, while also allowing us to identify and challenge them in the arguments of others. Often, fallacious thinkers present their positions with plausible—yet weak—evidence, appearing sincere and well-informed. However, their reasoning, much like a charlatan's act, is often rooted in false premises designed to mislead or confuse the unwary.

To combat this, it is essential to cultivate a keen awareness of logical fallacies and their manifestations. By doing so, we sharpen our critical thinking skills, building resilience against the allure of persuasive yet unsound arguments. Recognizing fallacies not only strengthens our reasoning but also empowers us to engage with others' arguments more effectively, fostering meaningful dialogue grounded in rationality and truth.

6

Applying Critical Thinking in Decision-Making

Critical thinking lies at the heart of effective decision-making, offering a framework that aligns strategic management, assessments, and organizational goals. As Stephen Covey highlighted in his work *The Speed to Results: How to Create a High-Performance Project* (1995), companies that prioritize objective thinking over mere result-oriented management gain a significant edge. Covey's insight underscores the transformative power of critical thinking in shaping organizational success.

One practical application of critical thinking is in aligning employee goals with company objectives, a process often referred to as **goal thinking**. By ensuring that the aspirations of workers complement the broader mission of the organization, businesses can cultivate a motivated, focused, and committed workforce. This alignment fosters mutually beneficial outcomes, where employees feel secure in their roles and organizations achieve their objectives. Even processes such as salary assessments, when informed by critical thinking, can reveal valuable insights into industry profiles and workforce dynamics.

Building a Culture of Critical Thinking

To truly harness the potential of critical thinking, it must be embedded in the company culture. A robust culture, paired with a well-defined strategic vision, forms the backbone of this endeavor. Strategic planning processes should undergo regular scrutiny and analysis, ensuring they remain adaptive and effective in meeting organizational goals. Healthy feedback loops play a pivotal role in this context, allowing businesses to measure key drivers against outcomes. Unfortunately, many organizations lack these continuous feedback mechanisms, which are crucial for fostering and sustaining a culture of critical thought.

Understanding the Impact of Critical Thinking

What distinguishes critical thinking from analytical, logical, or clear thinking? Why is it vital in business contexts? Critical thinking combines creativity and pragmatism, enabling organizations to navigate complex challenges with clarity and precision. It ensures that decisions are not based solely on whether something "works" but on whether it benefits all stakeholders involved.

Successful critical thinking involves two intertwined processes:

1. **Critical Thinking**: Rigorous questioning and evaluation of strategies and options based on evidence and feasibility.
2. **Creative Thinking**: The innovative generation of ideas and solutions to address challenges effectively.

Together, these processes empower organizations to resolve problems—big or small—with efficiency and foresight. For example, decisions such as hiring new employees, appointing task managers, or designing impactful campaigns all require a critical evaluation of options, alongside the creative capacity to envision and implement solutions.

A Call to Action

| 15 | – APPLYING CRITICAL THINKING IN DECISION-MAKING

Making critical thinking a priority transforms decision-making from a reactive process to a proactive strategy. It equips organizations to debate and question strategies, base decisions on realistic assessments, and adapt to evolving circumstances. By fostering a culture of critical thinking, companies can position themselves for long-term success while empowering individuals within the organization to contribute meaningfully.

7

Improving Creative Thinking

How can we observe people and situations more effectively? Developing creative thinking begins with sharpening our observational skills and cultivating a deeper awareness of the world around us. By embracing a mindful and systematic approach, we can radically shift the way we perceive and seek to understand others. Consider the following strategies to enhance your observational capacity and unlock creative insights:

1. **Identify the Key Actors and Their Roles** In any given situation, take a step back and assess who the participants are. What social roles or positions are they embodying? Which character archetypes might best describe their behavior—hero, antagonist, victim, scapegoat, or villain? Using a film or story analogy can provide a creative framework for interpreting their actions and motivations.
2. **Uncover the Motives Behind Behavior** Approach the situation like a detective, delving into the "why" behind people's actions. What drives their decisions or responses? Understanding their underlying motives offers valuable insights into their perspective and priorities, fostering a deeper appreciation of the dynamics at play.

3. **Analyze Body Language and Vocal Cues** Pay close attention to body language, as it often reveals emotions and intentions not explicitly stated. Listen carefully to the pitch, tone, and modulation of their voice. Does it tremble, rasp, or convey agitation? Observe facial expressions for subtle cues—are they controlled, strained, or unusually animated? These elements provide a wealth of information about someone's state of mind.
4. **Observe Physical Space and Movements** Note how individuals occupy and move within their physical space. Stress and heightened awareness can manifest in fluctuating movements: twitching fingers, rigid or uncoordinated head motions, shifts in posture, or decreased gestures. Ask yourself whether these physical cues are responses to environmental stimuli, efforts to reinforce an argument, or signs of deeper internal conflict.

By heightening our observational acuity, we can enrich our understanding of people and situations, paving the way for more creative and informed responses.

Historical Perspectives on Creative Thinking

In the 1930s, Alfred Sloan, then a leader at General Motors, encouraged managers to re-engage with reality through observation and thought. Sloan asserted, "Deeply engaging with what's real is in itself an extraordinary exercise in creative thinking. Let us seek and create the unknown future by engaging with it deeply every moment of every day." Similarly, Albert Einstein emphasized the importance of internal dialogue, advocating for direct, sensory-based learning as a catalyst for creativity. For Einstein, this intentional engagement was as vital as mathematical problem-solving in unlocking peak creativity.

The Creative Process: A Dialogue with Reality

The creative thinking process often unfolds as an internal dialogue—a unique interplay of ideas inspired by intentional observation and active engagement with our surroundings. Unfortunately, many of us engage with the world passively, using our eyes and ears with little deliberate effort. Creativity thrives when we develop the habit of paying attention to what others might overlook.

The Crucial Role of Perceptivity

Perceptivity—heightened observation of reality—is perhaps the most critical skill for fostering creativity. It requires us to resist the urge to jump to conclusions and instead immerse ourselves in the details of a situation. First impressions can often be misleading, especially when influenced by our energy levels, mood, or preconceived notions.

In both business and life, truth frequently lies beneath the surface. Observing the finer details, particularly subtle oddities that others may miss, can unlock extraordinary opportunities. These hidden observations often inspire innovative ideas and strategies that yield significant returns.

By cultivating perceptivity and embracing the small details, you position yourself to drive creative thinking that transforms challenges into opportunities. Engaging deeply with reality equips you to generate original ideas and solutions, ensuring lasting impact and success.

8

Overcoming Cognitive Biases

One of the simplest yet underutilized strategies for becoming aware of cognitive biases is to seek advice from others. Importantly, this advice should not be accepted as absolute truth—wisdom is a guide, not a rule. The value of advice lies not in blindly following it, but in carefully weighing it against your own reasoning and circumstances. Striking a balance between listening to diverse perspectives and evaluating their merit is crucial for navigating decision-making processes effectively.

When deliberating on any topic, particularly during policy formation, the input of a wide range of perspectives—including counter-arguments—is invaluable. This practice can serve as a safeguard against cognitive biases and outright mistakes, reducing the risk of judgments being clouded by the echo chamber of ideological support. While it's worth noting that others' reasoning may also be flawed, acknowledging and understanding potential biases is the first step toward mitigating their influence.

The Challenge of Altering Biases

Confronting deeply ingrained biases is a monumental challenge, yet it is an essential aspect of critical thinking. Cognitive biases distort our reasoning, cloud our judgment, and often lead us astray. Developing a deeper understanding of these mental shortcuts—what might be referred to as "mental hiccups"—is the foundation for improving critical thinking abilities.

Central to the goals of this book is the process of exposing and discussing these biases. Through self-reflection and introspection, these biases can gradually be overridden. While the complete elimination of biases may be unrealistic, incremental steps can help us move beyond simplistic and flawed thought patterns.

Among the most intractable biases are those that frequently surface during real-life, high-stakes decision-making. These include:

- **Over-interpretation**: Drawing excessive or unfounded conclusions from limited evidence.
- **Anchoring Effects**: Placing disproportionate weight on initial information when making decisions.
- **Emotionally Driven Biases**: Letting emotional reactions distort rational thinking.

Recognizing and addressing such biases is especially critical when tackling significant and challenging decisions.

Steps to Combat Cognitive Biases

To mitigate the influence of cognitive biases, consider adopting the following practices:

1. **Seek Diverse Perspectives**: Actively seek input from individuals with differing viewpoints. This can illuminate blind spots and challenge entrenched assumptions.
2. **Cultivate Self-Awareness**: Regularly reflect on your decision-making processes to identify patterns of bias.
3. **Engage in Deliberate Reflection**: Pause to evaluate the rationale behind your choices, ensuring they are based on evidence rather than impulse.

4. **Practice Mindful Introspection**: Be mindful of emotional reactions that may sway your reasoning, and consciously strive to separate feelings from facts.

By adopting these strategies, we can begin to uncover the biases that often operate beneath our conscious awareness. While biases may never be fully eradicated, these steps allow us to navigate decision-making processes with greater clarity, fairness, and rationality.

A Call to Action

Overcoming cognitive biases is not just a theoretical exercise—it's a skill that enhances our ability to think critically, reason effectively, and engage meaningfully with the world. The path to reducing bias requires effort, reflection, and a willingness to challenge our own assumptions. By committing to this journey, we not only strengthen our critical thinking abilities but also pave the way for more thoughtful, balanced, and impactful decisions.

9

Enhancing Communication Skills

Effective communication is a two-way process that demands not only persuasive speaking skills but also the ability to listen actively and attentively. Strong communication is rooted in mutual trust, respect, and empathy. By prioritizing meaningful conversations, building trust in others' ideas, and fostering an understanding of diverse perspectives, you can transform how you interact with the world.

Key Elements of Effective Communication

1. **Listening with Intent** Communication begins with listening—not just hearing words, but truly understanding the thoughts, feelings, and intentions behind them. Active listening demonstrates respect and encourages a deeper connection between individuals.
2. **Empathy and Trust** Developing empathy allows you to see the world through others' eyes, fostering trust and openness. This sensitivity to different communication styles—across cultures, generations, and contexts—enhances the richness of your interactions.

3. **Reflective Judgment** Before engaging in dialogue, pause to reflect on the potential impact of your words. Consider how your communication might influence your own growth as well as that of others. The most effective conversations are those that deepen the critical and reflective thinking skills of both the speaker and the listener.

Practical Strategies for Enhancing Communication

To cultivate and refine your communication abilities, consider the following approaches:

- **Stay Informed and Thoughtful** Engage in responsible discussions by becoming informed about important topics. However, go beyond simply presenting your viewpoint; critically evaluate others' perspectives before voicing your own.
- **Seek and Incorporate Feedback** Test your ideas by sharing them with those who disagree with you. Their feedback can serve as a valuable tool for refining your thoughts and improving your arguments.
- **Encourage Critical Thought** Stimulate thoughtful conversations by posing challenging questions and encouraging constructive feedback. Be willing to accept criticism as an opportunity for growth.
- **Acknowledge Complexity** Many important issues are nuanced and multifaceted. Avoid oversimplification; instead, ground your discussions in facts, principles, and theories. Recognizing complexity demonstrates intellectual integrity and respect for differing viewpoints.
- **Pursue Clarity and Coherence** Quality communication is well-structured, clear, and focused on substance. If your thoughts are not yet coherent, take time to apply critical

thinking skills before sharing them. Avoid the temptation to "win" arguments; instead, strive for impartial conflict resolution that prioritizes fairness and understanding.

Communication as a Tool for Growth

At its best, communication is a dynamic process that not only conveys ideas but also fosters personal and intellectual growth. Through dialogue, we refine our critical thinking skills, expand our understanding, and strengthen our connections with others. Effective communication is not about dominating the conversation but about creating space for collaborative exploration and mutual learning.

By implementing these strategies, you can enhance the quality of your interactions, make more meaningful contributions to discussions, and engage in communication that is both impactful and transformative.

10

Cultivating Curiosity and Open-Mindedness

When all else fails, there is one final and transformative option: pause and consider the possibility that you might have been wrong all along. Many people believe they can engage in fair-minded critical evaluations and arrive at reasoned conclusions. However, true critical thinking is not a singular event—it is a lifelong, holistic process that challenges and evolves with every new encounter and piece of information.

Critical thinking demands that we question even our most deeply held beliefs. For instance, rather than basing your worldview on a specific interpretation of a religious teaching, a political ideology, or a scientific theory, consider the possibility that these interpretations might have been influenced or shaped to serve self-serving, dictatorial, or power-seeking interests. If a belief or teaching cannot withstand rigorous critical evaluation, it may be rooted in familial, political, or institutional indoctrination rather than factual truth.

At its core, critical thinking is a good in itself—a practice essential to the ideals of a free society and the cultivation of a liberated mind. It calls for intellectual courage, flexibility, and the humility to admit when our understanding may need revision.

Breaking Free from Bias and Prejudice

Our thinking is often hindered by deeply ingrained biases and prejudices. These "sacred cows" manifest as strong, emotionally charged beliefs that we either fiercely defend or passionately embrace. When these attitudes remain unexamined, they block our ability to think objectively, detaching us from the pursuit of truth.

To overcome these mental barriers, we must remain open to modifying our beliefs, values, and theories in light of new evidence. Open-mindedness is not a passive state but an active effort to engage with diverse perspectives while maintaining a commitment to critical evaluation.

The Pillars of Open-Mindedness

1. **Respect for Diverse Opinions** Open-minded individuals accept and tolerate others' viewpoints, even when they strongly disagree with them. They recognize the importance of allowing everyone the freedom to express their ideas and expect the same courtesy in return.
2. **Rejection of Stereotypes** People who cultivate open-mindedness avoid stereotyping others, particularly those who belong to groups that might be perceived as different or unfamiliar. They strive to approach individuals without bias or preconceived notions.
3. **Willingness to Adapt** An open mind is flexible, willing to revise beliefs and assumptions based on new evidence. This adaptability is a hallmark of intellectual growth and maturity.

Curiosity as a Catalyst for Critical Thinking

Curiosity fuels the critical thinking process. When we actively seek to understand the world around us, we invite opportunities for learning and growth. Asking "why" and exploring the answers with an open mind helps dismantle rigid thought patterns and encourages innovative problem-solving.

By embracing curiosity and open-mindedness, we create a fertile ground for intellectual exploration and self-discovery. These qualities not only strengthen our capacity for critical thinking but also enrich our relationships, communication, and decision-making processes.

11

Utilizing Critical Thinking in Research and Analys

In the hypertext environment—an interconnected hypermedia structure that blends text, images, sound, and video—readers engage with information in fundamentally different ways compared to traditional, monomedia formats such as printed text. This dynamic environment reshapes how readers access topics, select and process sources, and ultimately present their findings. Unlike static texts, hypertext fosters a more interactive relationship between the reader and the material, influencing not only individual cognitive activity but also the broader design of web architecture, digital libraries, and scientific documents.

The Role of the Hypermedia Environment

The hypermedia environment significantly alters the cognitive and analytical processes involved in research. Readers interact with topics or sources in ways that resemble problem-solving mechanisms. For instance:

- Readers must navigate the digital landscape, using search strategies to locate and evaluate a diverse array of documents.
- They are required to process multimedia elements that demand simultaneous attention to various formats.

- Their cognitive input can even shape how hypertext is structured, affecting the design and functionality of digital platforms and scholarly resources.

This dynamic interaction underscores the evolving nature of research within digital ecosystems. Hypermedia has not only redefined traditional concepts of a digital library but also created an environment where user engagement drives the reconfiguration of information systems.

Insights from Current Studies

A growing body of research has explored how individuals consume and interact with information in hypermedia contexts. Studies on e-reading, e-learning, and information-seeking behaviors reveal that the hypertext format transforms the way people engage with information. Unlike traditional text, hypertext encourages a nonlinear exploration of ideas, fostering a unique interplay between cognitive strategies and technological design.

This chapter seeks to address critical questions regarding the influence of the hypermedia environment on knowledge users:

1. How does the hypertext format shape the way individuals think and process information?
2. What cognitive strategies do readers employ when navigating hypermedia documents?
3. How does the structure of hypertext impact the search for and synthesis of information?

By examining these questions, this analysis provides valuable insights into the interaction between reader cognition and digital environments.

Critical Thinking in Hypermedia Research

The mechanisms of information search within hypermedia environments closely align with the principles of critical thinking. Researchers must approach hypertext with deliberate strategies that include:

- Evaluating the reliability of diverse sources.
- Distinguishing between relevant and irrelevant information within a complex digital framework.
- Synthesizing multimedia elements to construct coherent conclusions.

Furthermore, critical thinking fosters adaptability in navigating the unique challenges of hypertext, such as fragmented narratives or overwhelming volumes of interconnected information.

Towards a Redefined Digital Landscape

Ultimately, the evolving role of hypermedia calls for a redefinition of digital libraries and research methodologies. Traditional, linear approaches to information must give way to more dynamic and integrative systems that reflect the interconnected nature of hypertext. This paradigm shift emphasizes the importance of critical thinking as a cornerstone for research in the digital age.

By understanding the cognitive and analytical dimensions of hypertext, researchers can harness its potential to enhance their thinking processes and contribute to more effective, innovative problem-solving.

12

Promoting Ethical Reasoning

Regardless of the context—family, professional settings, healthcare, or society—critical thinkers are called to approach ethical reasoning with profound respect for the wonderfully intricate web of human life choices. Ethical reasoning requires us to navigate blurred lines between moral rights and wrongs, delving deeply into our carefully cultivated systems of values and principles. It challenges our character, tests our courage, and sharpens our intellectual rigor.

Critical thinking in ethics is not only an intellectual exercise; it is a transformative process that educates, inspires, and leaves a lasting legacy for posterity. The inquiry itself offers a sense of fulfillment by urging us to constantly reevaluate our beliefs and actions, even in the face of doubt and moral ambiguity. It calls us to reason collectively, to act as role models, to foster empathy and understanding for others, to embrace habits of rational altruism, and to respect tradition and culture—all while reflecting critically on our own value systems.

Navigating Moral Dilemmas

Moral dilemmas often arise in the space where rights and obligations intersect. These situations demand the precision of critical thinking to foster peaceful coexistence. Ethical reasoning equips us to avoid the pitfalls of poorly executed group decisions—commonly referred to as "committee thinking." Whether in business, bioethics, or interpersonal conflicts, the critical question becomes: **How can all stakeholders be served?** While the answer may not always be straightforward, framing the dilemma through this lens encourages a balanced and equitable approach.

Ethical reasoning also prepares us to view problems from both objective and subjective perspectives, encouraging us to consider the broader context and underlying elements of an issue. This dual focus enhances our ability to make thoughtful, well-informed decisions.

The Interconnection of Morality and Decision-Making

Ethical reasoning in education and life inevitably flows along two interconnected paths—the moral high road and the moral low road. These paths are intertwined, with one shaping and evolving from the other. Every decision we make is informed—or potentially misinformed—by our own ethical framework. We view problems through the lens of our moral reflections, working to disentangle logic from ethical considerations. This process allows us to critically evaluate decisions with clarity and balance, weighing both factual and moral aspects.

Even when decisions involve multiple evaluative criteria, ethical considerations are always present. Developing the ability to distinguish between logical reasoning and moral imperatives is the hallmark of a critical thinker. It provides the time and space needed to weigh the significance of each aspect according to the evidence and principles at hand. This detached perspective enhances higher-level thinking and minimizes the likelihood of irrational conflicts.

A Call to Higher Ethical Standards

Ethical reasoning grows from an understanding and integration of the many layers of our personality into our decision-making processes. It reflects our finest human qualities—integrity, empathy, and intellectual honesty. By striving to promote ethical reasoning in both individual and collective contexts, we demonstrate our commitment to fostering thoughtful, compassionate, and responsible societies.

Promoting ethical reasoning is not just about making decisions; it is about cultivating the ability to think critically, reflect deeply, and act with integrity. It invites us to approach each moral challenge not as an obstacle, but as an opportunity to embody our highest values and ideals.

13

Fostering Collaborative Thinking

Collaborative thinking elevates cognitive processes to a higher level, enabling individuals and teams to create innovative operational procedures, develop groundbreaking products, and forge meaningful business connections. At its core, collaboration thrives on active thinking skills that spark creativity and problem-solving. Conflict, when approached constructively, can lead to new ideas, refined procedures, and stronger teamwork.

The Role of Self-Critical Evaluation

The collaborative process often involves the evolution of ideas. The original concept may not survive in its initial form, but peer feedback and collective evaluation serve to validate or improve upon it. This self-critical evaluation is a cornerstone of teamwork, fostering creativity and enhancing outcomes.

To fully embrace collaboration, it is essential to set aside egotistical drives, as these can be counterproductive to cooperation. While recognition and praise are natural desires, a true professional thinker substitutes external validation with self-discipline and internal evaluation. Knowing you've contributed effectively should be its own reward, and any external praise should be regarded as a marker of efficiency, not a necessity.

The Importance of Maintaining an Open Mind

Defensiveness can be a barrier to collaboration. When individuals feel threatened and become defensive, they risk shutting down communication—not only for themselves but for the entire team. Instead, adopting a team-oriented approach can yield win-win solutions.

Key principles of effective teamwork include:

- **Equal Participation**: Ensuring everyone has their turn to contribute and is genuinely listened to.
- **Synergy**: Combining the unique strengths and ideas of team members to achieve outcomes far greater than any single individual's contribution.
- **Constructive Conflict**: Recognizing that disagreement, when managed respectfully, can deepen understanding and improve decision-making.

When differing views are shared, ideas are challenged and strengthened through further explanation and justification. Avoiding or glossing over conflict can hinder shared understanding and prevent the group from fully embracing a final decision. Disagreement is healthy when it remains focused on the issue at hand and avoids assigning negative motives to individuals.

Achieving Healthy Interpersonal Dynamics

Synergy emerges when people genuinely collaborate, building upon one another's ideas to achieve shared goals. The process deepens participants' thinking skills and strengthens interpersonal relationships. Collaboration doesn't require unanimous agreement—it thrives on diversity of thought. However, flexibility and respect are crucial to ensuring that differences enhance, rather than hinder, progress.

By fostering an environment where differing perspectives are encouraged and disagreements are depersonalized, teams can create solutions that are not only innovative but also inclusive and sustainable.

Building Toward Collaborative Success

Collaboration is not just about achieving a single result; it is about creating a culture of openness, creativity, and mutual respect. By letting go of egotism, embracing feedback, and remaining open to differing ideas, individuals can contribute to a collective effort that surpasses individual contributions.

In this way, fostering collaborative thinking becomes more than a skill—it becomes a mindset that enriches both personal and professional endeavors.

14
Applying Critical Thinking in Everyday Life

Sophisticated critical reasoning is not confined to a single discipline, lecture, group, text, or institution. It is cultivated through consistent, interdisciplinary education that transforms information into practical alternatives. The journey of mastering critical thinking requires an active and ongoing effort to connect ideas across diverse contexts and disciplines, applying them in meaningful ways to real-life situations.

The Role of Education in Critical Thinking

Research underscores the vital role of the educational community in fostering critical thinking. This involves two core objectives:

1. **Integrating a Mental Approach to Critical Thinking**: Encouraging students to develop the mindset of a critical thinker, equipping them to approach problems with intellectual rigor.
2. **Enhancing Long-Term Learning Outcomes**: Designing courses and teaching methods that emphasize the significance of critical thinking, empowering students to better understand and apply concepts over the long term.

Educators, from introductory levels to advanced university courses, play a pivotal role in this process. They serve as critical thinkers, problem-solvers, and reflective learners, modeling these qualities to inspire and guide their students. When classrooms foster a learning environment that incorporates effective teaching approaches, both educators and students benefit from enhanced interaction and engagement. For example, teachers might:

- Challenge their own thoughts and ask students to critically assess conclusions.
- Encourage students to resolve the core nature of problems rather than simply answer questions.
- Incorporate scientific strategies in laboratory or real-world settings to deepen understanding.

Real-Life Applications of Critical Thinking

The true value of critical thinking lies in its application to complex, real-life circumstances. By studying critical thinking, individuals learn not only to outline theoretical processes and models but also to apply these frameworks effectively in personal, regional, national, or global contexts. Students who master critical thinking can:

- Assess data and information systematically and objectively.
- Draw empirical conclusions grounded in evidence.
- Present well-reasoned solutions to controversial or multifaceted issues.

Critical thinking also requires acknowledging one's cognitive weaknesses and presuppositions—a liberating yet challenging process. Recognizing these limitations eliminates the possibility of appealing to ignorance or blind acceptance. Instead, it cultivates a heightened awareness of one's own thought processes, creating opportunities for growth and self-improvement.

Addressing Cognitive Biases and Complexity

Understanding the psychological foundations of biases—whether environmental, genetic, or both—forms a critical component of critical thinking. Awareness of these traits, often studied through research in psychology, enables individuals to employ strategies to mitigate biases and engage more effectively in learning and decision-making.

By embracing knowledge with the depth and complexity it requires, students and thinkers alike are better equipped to challenge traditional models and explore innovative approaches. This process mirrors the complexity of real-life problems, offering tools to approach issues with nuance and creativity.

The Empowering Nature of Knowledge

Critical thinking transforms knowledge into a powerful tool for navigating life's challenges. It empowers individuals to approach topics with intellectual depth, challenge established norms, and refine their understanding of the world. By fostering critical awareness and embracing the complexity of real-world problems, individuals develop the capacity to engage with confidence, clarity, and purpose in both professional and personal contexts.

Enjoyed This Book? Let Others Know!

If this book has blessed, encouraged, or challenged you in any way, I'd love to hear about it! Your review not only helps others discover this message but also encourages me to keep writing.

Would you take a moment to share your thoughts? A few sentences on what stood out to you can make a big difference.

You can leave a review on Amazon, Goodreads, or wherever you purchased this book. Thank you for being part of this journey!

www.ingramcontent.com/pod-product-compliance
Lightning Source LLC
LaVergne TN
LVHW041641070526
838199LV00052B/3485

tial. It guards against the harm we might inflict on ourselves and others through hasty judgments or unchecked biases. It challenges us to remain vigilant in the pursuit of truth, even when faced with complex or contentious issues.

The consequences of neglecting critical thinking extend beyond the personal realm. Violations of sound reasoning can perpetuate social injustice, fuel civil unrest, and erode the foundations of cooperative progress. By contrast, the exercise of critical faculties becomes a tool for justice, understanding, and peace.

A Call to Action

This book has been an invitation to become a more thoughtful, vigilant reasoner—someone equipped to navigate the challenges of a rapidly changing world while safeguarding integrity and fairness. Critical thinking is not simply about avoiding pitfalls; it is about aspiring to the highest ideals of intellectual and moral excellence.

As you move forward, consider the role critical thinking will play in your personal journey. Reflect on its potential to inform your decisions, shape your relationships, and inspire action toward a more just and compassionate society. The practice of critical thinking is not just about solving problems; it is about embodying the best of what it means to be human.

Conclusion

As we conclude this chapter, let us reflect on a familiar but enduring challenge to critical thinking: the danger of succumbing to the persuasive ubiquity of power. In moments where societal forces seek to obscure truth, it is imperative to uphold moral, intellectual, and spiritual courage. By applying critical thinking in service of a vulnerable society, we contribute collectively to one of the most powerful forces for justice and peace the world has ever known.

Critical thinking is not merely an academic exercise—it holds the potential to profoundly transform our lives. Beyond addressing practical problems, it touches the innermost concerns of the human spirit. Through this volume, we have explored critical thinking not just as an intellectual process but as a means of enriching both personal and collective lives.

Revisiting the Foundation of Critical Thinking

In Chapter 1, we introduced fundamental ideas surrounding critical thinking. Now, with a broader and deeper understanding, we return to the question: **What is critical thinking, and why does it matter?**

Some have doubted its significance, questioning whether it truly has the power to shape lives meaningfully. However, as we have seen throughout this book, critical thinking is the practice of using specific skills to inquire into beliefs, notions, and realities. This process empowers individuals to shape their lives responsibly and meaningfully, fostering clarity, growth, and truth.

The Urgency of Critical Thinking in Modern Life

In a world inundated with irrelevant, confusing, incomplete, and often false information—whether from airwaves, written media, or digital platforms—critical thinking is not just important; it is essen-